For my son D.G.
and Ashby Willesley
Primary School

C.T.

For the children of
Bingham Kindergarten

S.G.

I Don't Want To!

by Sally Grindley
Illustrated by Carol Thompson

JOY STREET BOOKS

Little, Brown and Company
Boston Toronto London

When Mom came in and said
it was time to get up, Jim said,
"I don't want to,"
and hid under the sheets.

When Dad came up to help him
put on his brand-new clothes,
Jim said, "I don't want to,"
and made himself all arms and legs.

When Mom gave him his egg and
said he must eat it before he went out,
Jim said, "I don't want to,"
and threw his toast on the floor.

When Dad put on his coat and
said it was time for them to go,
Jim said, "I don't want to."
But he had to.

"You'll enjoy it," said Dad.

"You'll have fun," said Mom.

"Won't," said Jim.

When they got into the car,
Jim said, "I want to go home."

When they drove up to the school,
Jim said, "I want to go home."

When they walked into the classroom,
Jim said, "I want to go home."
But he couldn't.
"Hello, Jim," said Miss Jones,
"come and sit with Jenny and Paul."
"I don't want to," said Jim.
"I want to go home."

"We're going to do some painting," said
Miss Jones. "Don't you want to join in?"
"No," said Jim, "I want to go home."

Miss Jones got out the paints and brushes.
The children put their aprons on.
    Miss Jones laid down a great big
sheet of paper. The children started
to color it in.

Jim sat at his table and
tried very hard not to listen.
Jim sat at his table and
tried very hard not to watch.
But he couldn't help thinking that
what they were doing looked fun.
He couldn't help wishing that
he was doing it too.

He couldn't help standing and saying, "I want to do that."

Miss Jones was very pleased.

Jim joined in with the painting

and he joined in with the songs.

He joined in with the reading

and he joined in with the dancing.

He joined in with the counting

and he joined in with the games.

When Mom came to collect him
and said it was time to go home,
Jim said, "I don't want to."
But he had to.

Then Miss Jones said,
  "You can come back tomorrow."
The children said,
  "Come back tomorrow, Jim."

And Jim wanted to.

Text Copyright © 1990 by Sally Grindley
Illustrations Copyright © 1990 by Carol Thompson
Published in Great Britain in 1990 by Methuen Children's Books

First U.S. Edition

Library of Congress Catalog Card Number 89-85798

10 9 8 7 6 5 4 3 2 1

Joy Street Books are published by
Little, Brown and Company (Inc.)

Printed in Belgium by
Proost International Book Production